Building High-Performance Teams

Why Clarity, Alignment and Trust are The Pillars to Building a Team that Wins

LUIS RAUL SCOTT, JR.

© 2024 Luis Raul Scott, Jr.

ISBN: 979-8-32240-313-5 (pb)

Typesetting: Scott Publishing Services

ALL RIGHTS RESERVED. This book contains material protected under International and Federal Copyright Laws and Treaties. Any unauthorized reprint or use of this material is prohibited. No part of this book may be reproduced or transmitted in any form or by any means, electronic or mechanical, including photocopying, recording, or by any information storage and retrieval system without express written permission of the publisher, except in the case of brief quotations embodied in critical reviews and certain noncommercial uses permitted by copyright law. For permissions requests, write to the publisher, addressed "Attention: Permissions Request," to scottpublishingservices@gmail.com.

Table of Contents

Introduction
Building High-Performance Teams................... 7

Chapter 1
The Ultimate Leader Approach........................13

Chapter 2
How to Recognize Under-Performing Teams.. 19

Chapter 3
What does it mean to be high performing?.... 29

Chapter 4
Understanding Team Types............................. 41

Chapter 5
Team Member Values....................................... 51

Chapter 6
Earning Trust... 59

Chapter 7
Clarity and Communication.............................. 67

Chapter 8
Developing Leadership.....................................73

Chapter 9
Team Building..79

Conclusion.. 83

Introduction
Building High-Performance Teams

"Talent wins games, but teamwork and intelligence win championships."

– Michael Jordan

Michael Jordan was undoubtedly the greatest basketball player of all time, unless of course you are a Lebron James fan. Despite his incredible success as a player, Jordan could not have won 6 championships on his own. The championships, which made him a true idol, were part of a team effort.

Just like in sports, high-performance teams are crucial to the success of any business. Whether you're a large or mid-size firm, if your teams aren't performing at an optimum level, you're losing at least some of your return on investment. Think about it. You've put countless hours of blood, sweat, tears, and dollars into building your business, and every ounce of underperformance is a waste of your hard work. High-performance teams propel businesses into the stratosphere of success. Without them, you can't achieve much. With them, anything is possible.

Several years ago, I was at a conference learning about the power of a unified team. In this example, the presenter showed a picture of a horse and carriage. There was nothing unique about this horse. He started talking about how the horse could pull a carriage in a single day approximately 15 to 20 miles. He then also started talking about the amount of weight that the horse and carriage could pull. He said that one horse in a single day would be able to pull approximately 8,000 lbs. for those 15 to 20 miles. To me, that seemed pretty impressive when you think about the weight of the carriage and possibly the people riding inside of the carriage. And then he pulled out another picture. This picture had two horses and the same carriage. He then asked the audience a question, "How much do you think that two horses can pull?" The obvious answer was 8,000 times 2 for a total of 16,000 lbs. But that would have been wrong. He then presented the next slide and the number was actually astronomically larger than 16,000 lbs. Two horses could pull over 30,000 lbs. depending on the breed of horse and they could do for up to 40 miles.

To me this illustrated an incredibly powerful story of unity and teamwork. The more unified that your team is, the more committed your team is, the clearer your team is, the more aligned your team is, and the more trust that your team shows to each other, will create an astronomical outcome in your business. The weight that this high performing team can pull and the distance to which it can pull it, is significantly greater than one person doing it alone.

> *Successful businesses don't come with ready-made teams performing at the upper echelon of their talent.*

And I hear this all the time as I'm coaching and consulting companies around the country, and that is that everybody wants an A player. And I don't disagree with the desire of wanting the best of the best. But when you are competing to attract the best of the best you will find that there is always another company out there so desperate to pay that person a premium that you're not capable of paying. So, I've always coached my clients to not simply look for the best of the best employees to work in your organization, although that is a very important thing to do. But to also look at how you can assemble a team of driven, aligned, trustworthy employees that can help you develop a system that allows you to carry the weight and allows you to go the distance of a 2-horse drawn carriage instead of A 1-horse drawn carriage.

Because all too often we believe that just one person is going to transform our organization completely and radically. And even if that was the case, that person, just like the single horse, will get tired at some point if they are not surrounded by a team of people that can strengthen them and elevate them day in and day out.

In this book about building high-performance teams, I'll discuss the following:

- How to spot underperforming teams
- What it means to have high-performing teams
- The various team-types
- Why high-performing teams have aligned values
- How to make trust the foundation of your teams
- Reducing clarity concerns in high-performing teams
- Communication breakdowns and why they matter
- Leaders and team building as cornerstones of high-performing teams

Successful businesses don't come with ready-made teams performing at the upper echelon of their talent. Like anything, managers must carefully construct these teams, periodically reconfiguring their arrangement. Once one or more teams are performing well, you can't just sit back and give them free reign. Sure, you can step away to a degree, but remember that, as the primary leader, you're an integral part of these teams and you owe them your attention. There is no such thing as set it and forget it when it comes to working with people. One day when you have enough leaders you can use the set it and forget it strategy. This becomes easier to do once you reach around $10 million in yearly revenue because you can actually begin to afford those A players that you so desperately want.

People are the most complicated part of growing a business because they all have minds, desires and upbringings that generally depart from those of the leader and the owner. Learning how to sync up the individual vision and the business vision is a work of art that takes time and effort.

One of the first things you'll learn in this book is how to recognize the warning signs of a team that isn't performing well. Many firm owners or employee managers are shocked to find they've missed the red flags or attributed workplace issues to something other than team cohesion. Since external factors you can't control can sometimes result in similar dysfunction—including the state of the economy, pandemic-related shifts in consumer habits, and natural disasters—we'll talk about how you can tell the difference.

People looking to turn their businesses into fine-tuned machines can use this book as a guide, whether they need a tune-up or need to learn how to build high-performing teams from scratch. The Ultimate Leadership Toolkit Series, of which this book is one part of that series, is designed to provide a blueprint for your route to success. Regardless of where you are on your business journey, this book can become a valuable resource for you and the leaders on your team.

While this book is for everyone, entrepreneurs with a fire under them to get the job done will get the most out of it. If you're motivated to do the work, and you want to grow your business using some of the best advice out there, you've come to the right spot. Keep reading to learn how you can build the high-performance teams you need to get the job done right.

Chapter 1
The Ultimate Leader Approach

"People do not decide to become extraordinary. They decide to accomplish extraordinary things."

– Edmund Hillary

I always had the drive to do something great. One of my greatest fears was that I would die, and my life would not count for anything. It sounds kind of morbid to think about when you are 11 years old but that's where my mind was at the time. I never set out to be meaningful but rather I wanted to do meaningful things. I wanted to invent something or come up with something that changed people's lives. I could not have imagined it would have been a signature business growth formula but that's what it was.

I was convinced at a young age that leadership was the key to extraordinary wealth and an extraordinary life. Growing up in a humble home from a financial standpoint gave me all the drive I needed to do something different in my life. I wanted the best that the world could offer. I knew that it required me to grow as an individual so that I would be qualified to earn the money I wanted sometime in my lifetime.

Knowing this, when I started writing this book series, I really wanted to answer one question, "How do I become the ultimate leader?" If leadership was the secret, then becoming the ultimate leader was the answer. One of the primary responsibilities of the Ultimate Leader is to guide and develop high performing team. If you are looking to be an ultimate leader, you have to become really good at leading and developing high performance teams.

A mentor of mine one time told me that the mark of a leader is based on his or her following. If you claim to be a leader and no one is following, you are simply taking a walk. Don't get me wrong, I love walks. But that's not the goal for the ultimate leader. You must be at the forefront of the team.

My Story

Before we dive into our core ideas, I want to spend the first chapter outlining my path to success so you can understand not only why I want to share my knowledge but also why you can trust the roadmap I've laid out. I spent years working my way through the ranks of a successful, multi-million-dollar business. I started out as a part-time interpreter and receptionist, and after a decade, I was the managing partner at that same firm. Climbing the ladder, as I did, allowed me to see and understand businesses in ways few other partner-level attorneys are able to. I learned how businesses operate, or fail to operate, with hands-on experience by working in almost every position in the firm.

Eventually, I began wondering if there was a better way to do things. At the time, I didn't have as much control over firm operations as I would have liked, and I knew I wanted to steer my own ship. Even though I was already a successful attorney, something deep down told me there was more to my career. Ultimately, that voice deep inside grew until I finally made the leap and started my own business after leaving my partnership.

> *If you claim to be a leader and no one is following, you are simply taking a walk.*

During the 15 years I was at my first firm, I spent countless hours developing myself through books, videos and conferences. Between traditional books and summaries, I have read almost 600 books. Each one taught me something new or reinforced something I already knew. Most importantly, they provided so many different perspectives on what worked and didn't work when it came to leading people.

After leaving that firm, through a series of good decisions, what I started from scratch grew my firm from nothing to over $30 million in annual revenue in five years. You might wonder how any of this applies to a book about high-performance teams. Well, during those five years, our employee and contractor count rose almost to 200 people. It was through that explosive people growth that I learned the importance of building high performing teams. I have seen it all and tried it all when it comes to putting together the best and most efficient teams, and I'm writing this book to pass along the information I've found most helpful.

The short cut to success is your people. And there is no shortcut to the shortcut.

Since achieving this success, I have been teaching others to build their own firms to 8 Figures in predictable revenue using my signature growth formula. Building an 8-Figure Firm requires more than aggressive marketing skills. In addition to developing leads and an excellent referral network, people wanting to grow their business and firms quickly need to learn how to manage all the personalities involved. As they say, "teamwork makes the dream work." Unless you can make that dream work, you're not going to achieve the growth you need to meet your needs. And that is why I've written this book.

All too often people believe that the sheer grit that they used in building their business to $1 million or even maybe $3 million can somehow take them to $10 million+. But this is just not the case. To build a business that is sufficient in size to actually operate on its own, you will need to master the art of building teams. Teams will run your business. As I often tell my clients, the short cut to success is your people. And there is no shortcut to the shortcut.

Over the course of this book, I'm going to lay out a roadmap that discusses:

- Recognizing and understanding high performance
- Team-types
- Values
- Trust
- Clarity and Communication
- Leadership
- Team Building

Each of these items must be addressed before you can build teams that will operate on the level needed to help you grow a business that not only accomplishes something extraordinary but that also meets the needs of your life.

Chapter Takeaway

The bigger you want to grow your business, the more you have to develop yourself. On your own, you may be able to do a lot, but you will not be able to accomplish as much as you could leading a team. You cannot have a meaningful impact with your business if you do not develop your teams to becoming high performance machines. High performance machines require the operator's input. Neglecting the development of your teams will cause stagnation in your business and will result in under performance. Never underestimate the power of a unified team.

Effective team building requires understanding the people you bring on board and how everyone's values, culture, communication skills, and leadership abilities interact to form a team. At times, to better understand if and where team breakdowns are occurring, you'll need to perform both internal and external analyses of the entire system.

Chapter 2
How to Recognize Under-Performing Teams

"Mistakes are always forgivable, if one has the courage to admit them."

– Bruce Lee

During the economic downturn of 2008-2009, Ford was facing significant challenges. Ford recognized that one of its key divisions, the Lincoln-Mercury brand, was underperforming compared to competitors in the luxury car market, such as BMW and Mercedes-Benz.

CEO Alan Mulally, conducted a thorough analysis of the situation and recognized several key issues contributing to the underperformance of the Lincoln-Mercury brand: **Product Lineup**, **Brand Perception** and **Internal Culture**.

There were also internal cultural challenges within Ford, including siloed departments and a resistance to change, which hindered the company's ability to innovate and adapt to market demands. Employees were not working as teams seeking the best results but rather as individuals.

To address these issues and revitalize the Lincoln-Mercury brand, Ford implemented a comprehensive turnaround strategy that focused on **Investment in Product Development**, **Rebranding and Marketing Efforts and Cultural Transformation**.

The biggest of the three was the cultural transformation which focused on collaboration, transparency, and accountability. This cultural shift helped break down silos within the organization and fostered a more agile and innovative mindset.

These efforts paid off. Ford launched successful new vehicles under the Lincoln brand, such as the Lincoln MKZ and MKX, and eventually launched other vehicles that continued to expand the luxury appeal of the Ford Company.

Many times, when I coach clients, the first thing I hear is that their team is underperforming. As with Ford, this may actually be true. Yet, when I ask them why they believe this, they can never give me data that supports the belief. They just **feel** like the team is underperforming.

Several years ago, I was working with a client who continued to tell me his team was underperforming. When we did a deep dive into the business, we found that the average revenue per employee was consistently over $250,000 in revenue, profit was over 20% and the business was growing 50%+ year over year for the past 5 years. I couldn't understand the constant complaining about the business. So where did the feeling of underperformance come from?

It's not always easy to recognize an underperforming team. But this skill is essential in building much-desired and necessary high-performing teams. Before you can improve a team's performance, you need to recognize where and how it's underperforming. The signs aren't always initially obvious, but if you pay attention, you can learn to see the red flags. When you know how to spot the signs of poor performance in your teams, you'll be able to stop the downward spiral and start on a path of improvement.

Here are the red flags we found after we did a deep dive. The solutions then became obvious.

Red Flag No. 1: Client Complaints and Terminations

The first red flag we saw was the business was experiencing client terminations. In one year, my client had received 75 terminations of their clients. Something was definitely wrong here. Over the years you're in business, you'll lose clients for a variety of reasons: maybe they don't like your company culture, or maybe they think they can get a better deal somewhere else.

The performance of your teams usually has nothing to do with it. Usually—underperforming teams can and do drive clients away if their work is poor enough or their culture toxic enough, or if they repeatedly miss their deadlines. Asking for feedback when clients end their relationship with you is an excellent way to get to the root of their dissatisfaction. But too many terminations is always a reflection of underperforming teams.

One easy giveaway that your teams aren't performing well is that you'll start receiving client complaints. If there is an increase in customer complaints, that means that the client is either not receiving the service and outcomes that they want from your product or business or that the customer service and response times are lacking.

These complaints will come through phone calls and emails and usually disguised as an upset client. Additionally you may start seeing more negative reviews online or possibly just as bad, no reviews at all. One way to solve this is to be proactive in getting customer feedback before the client has a chance of complaining. Often, a client would rather complain to you in person than through a public review, so if you give them that option, there's a smaller chance of harming your online ratings. The bottom line is that client satisfaction is often the canary in the coal mine of team performance.

Red Flag No. 2: Missed Deadlines

The second red flag we saw when I looked into my client's complaints was that his team was often missing deadlines. In fact in just a matter of 6 months his company had received multiple complaints with the governing body of the state for ethical violations related to missed deadlines and had also received a couple of malpractice claims for legal malpractice. So yes most cases were being processed quickly, but their were signs.

Some additional missed deadlines that can be under the radar and not as easy to spot include:

- Not calling the client back timely
- Not responding to emails timely
- Not filing paperwork timely
- Not sending quotes to client timely
- Not finishing a project timely

When you begin to see any of these things pop up in the day to day work of the individual clients, you know that someone on the team is underperforming in their work.

Red Flag No. 3: Poor Work Quality

The third red flag we saw when we looked deep into the work was that the quality of the representation was suffering. In most industries a standard exists as to the value of each individual client is worth to the business. Some call this the lifetime value of the client. The better you serve the client, the more likely it is that the lifetime value will be higher. A lower lifetime value is generally a sign of poor quality.

One of the easiest ways to illustrate this is comparing the company Nike to Payless shoes. Although you can likely purchase more pairs of shoes buying at payless, the quality and comfort of Nike is superior. Because of this, people spend 10's of thousands of dollars buying shoes from Nike and generally Payless is a last resort type of purchase. The reason is that the quality matters when it comes to raising the lifetime values of your clients.

In observation we immediately saw that there was a dip in the lifetime values of each client by almost $2,000 per client. When looking under the hood even more, we realized that there were some producers (lawyers) who were just not producing and getting mediocre results on the cases.

Poor quality is something that is hard to find sometimes unless you are actively doing a comparative analysis department wide. Many times, poor work quality is be something you don't notice until a client brings it to your attention, but hopefully, you catch it before it makes it out the door and into the client's hands. Some easy ways to spot poor quality is to check the objective work. Meaning look at the physical output and see if you would rate it as excellent work.

Just as it takes a team to produce high-quality work product, it takes a team to allow work product with errors and omissions to pass through your checkpoint systems. Planes don't crash when only one thing goes wrong, the experts say; instead, several problems have to pass quality checkpoints without resolution before a plane crash occurs. This metaphor extends to any workplace. The end product you send to your clients is always a result of teams, whether they're high-performing or underperforming.

Be sure to create audit systems for your team so that you can stay abreast to the work that is being produced and the quality that is being produced.

Red Flag No. 4: In-House Arguing

The fourth red flag that we saw was infighting between employees. Leaders and the team were not on the same page. And remember, all of this was happening while delivering what appeared on paper is good results. Multiple employees had quit because of a "toxic" leader. Several attorneys quit with no notice because of perceived micromanagement. Complaints of favoritism ran rampant, and no one was working to resolve these issues in a proactive manner.

A toxic environment is another symptom of underperforming teams. Conflict occurs when some team members become upset that deadlines are being missed or work quality is below standard. While it's great that you have some team members who want to course correct, arguing won't solve your problem. This is a leadership problem: you need to step in and take the reins or appoint a new team leader to steer the ship at whatever level the breakdown is occurring.

> *A toxic environment is another symptom of underperforming teams.*

Findings

In the end we found what my client was looking for- evidence that his team was underperforming. But it was no longer a feeling and we had objective proof that it was happening. The next steps were to try to figure out how to fix it all. This was a task that required almost two years of work as we created better systems and replaced people who no longer fit the new culture of the organization. Despite record numbers and profit, my client was right to think his team was underperforming and now we knew why.

Chapter Takeaways

Underperformance can lead to a variety of objective red flags. To spot them, ask the question, "Where is my team missing the mark?" If you find that the team is missing the mark, it is likely that they are underperforming. Do not be susceptible to the thought that simply because you are growing and have a decent profit margin that your teams are doing well. They could be winning on the big items and losing on the micro parts of the business. Like water, it only takes a drop for an extended period of time for it to corrode metal. Do not allow little things to become disruptive forces in your organization. Be on the lookout for signs your teams aren't performing as well as they should be, and telescope in on the root issues so you can find solutions at that level. Whenever possible, solicit client feedback, which can help you identify problems.

Chapter 3
What does it mean to be high performing?

"If we did the things we were capable of, we would astound ourselves."

– Thomas Edison

For many years I have come home from work and my wife has asked me, "How was work today?" I usually say some variation of "It was fine." What I really wanted to say was, "I only put in 70% effort and I wish I could get myself to put 100% every day. Imagine where I would be."

She has now heard me say things and always tells me I am just too hard on myself. But I know what it looks like to be a high performer and I know what it takes to be at the top of your game. When I think about Edison's statement, I believe it to be true. We would absolutely astound ourselves if we just did the things we were capable of.

In the most recent past I took on this challenge and this book that you are reading is the outcome of putting in the hard work and effort to astound myself. It is a collection of leadership principles that will be finished at over 1,000 pages of materials just on leadership. Took me almost 40 years to figure this out.

But what is high performance?

The Dream Team

I'm sure more people have heard the story of the "Dream Team". The 1992 United States men's basketball team, famously known as the "Dream Team" will go down in history as one of the greatest sports stories of all time. Prior 1992, NBA players were prohibited from playing in the Olympics despite other countries having the luxury of their professional teams playing. When the USA basketball Association asked the NBA to provide talent to the Olympic team, they were initially very hesitant.

Eventually the team was assembled, and it included legends such as Michael Jordan, Magic Johnson, Larry Bird, Charles Barkley, Karl Malone, Scottie Pippen, Patrick Ewing, David Robinson, and many more. 11 of the 12 players selected for the Dream Team went on to be inducted into the Basketball Hall of Fame. That is absolutely insane and an incredible line up of superstars.

The Dream Team went undefeated throughout the tournament. They won every game by an average

What does it mean to be high performing?

margin of 44 points. The objective metrics were very clear on their performance.

The Dream Team's participation in the Olympics had a profound impact on the international popularity of basketball. Basketball was elevated worldwide because of the team.

They became a symbol of American excellence. Their dominance transcended basketball and left an enduring imprint on popular culture.

What was evident about the Dream Team is that high performing teams don't just win, they crush the competition.

> *Teams performing at the best of their abilities can set and stick to defined objectives.*

Since I mentioned the word competition, I don't want to get too far into this section without being crystal clear, I don't believe in competition. Read my books on marketing to understand why. But I do believe that whatever we deem to be competition is eventually left in the dust when you are working with high performance teams. These teams just crush everything and everybody. You feel good about them. You know they have what it takes to run without you. They have synergy, energy and positive vibes. They remind you how much fun it can be to be an entrepreneur.

Before building a high-performance team, you need to know what the term means. Most people believe "performance" and "success" mean the same thing, but they are not. As I discussed in the preceding chapter, the outcome of your team's performance could be bad or good. In the case of high-performing teams, you're likely to experience the following results: record-breaking client retention and increased revenue. When everyone is performing at their peak, the only direction to move is up! High-performance teams operate efficiently, with clearly defined objectives. They're simultaneously operating across functions, and you should be able to measure consistent, increased success. There is greater clarity, alignment and trust which are the essentially of developing these high performing teams. Clarity provides the roadmap, alignment provides the buy in, trust is the glue that holds everything and everyone together.

Let's take a more granular look at the elements I believe to be the four cornerstones of high performance: **defined objectives, maximized efficiency, cross-functionality, and measurable success**.

Defined Objectives

At the end of 2022 I was working with a business that had set their sights on achieving the illustrious $1 million in revenue per month. This is a huge milestone. It is essentially a virtual guarantee that the owner will take home at least 7 figures in personal income. She was determined to hit it. Here was the "problem" I saw. At the time she was only generating around $250,000 in revenue per month. I just didn't see how she was going to make that sort of leap. Me being the financially conservative coach that I was, I asked her to really explore if that was a possibility in such a short period of time.

She was adamant that this objective was going to be met no matter what and she was going to make it happen. Less than 18 months later it happened. Not only that it happened month after month after month and now as of our last talk she was on pace to do $15 million in revenue in 2024 and $30 million in the next two years. There is nothing more powerful than a defined objective when working with teams. The primary objective that helped the team propel to this incredible success started at the very top.

Teams performing at the best of their abilities can set and stick to defined objectives. Of course, this can be easier said than done, as a defined objective requires decision-making, organization, agreement, and delegation. If your teams can define their objectives, they're well on their way to success. Defining the team objectives starts with defining the organizational objectives first. The organizational objective comes from the leadership.

If your team has difficulties defining their objectives, or sticking to the objective they've defined, don't be discouraged. After all, that's why you're reading this book, right? Take it one step at a time. You should poll the team and ask them to assess the quality of their processes:

- Are they struggling with goal setting?
- Are they struggling with agreeing on what goals to set?
- Do they have a clear leader to delegate tasks associated with the objectives?
- Have they defined the who does what by when?
- Is there a communication breakdown?

Once you identify the primary culprit behind your team's failure to set and complete objectives, you'll have removed a significant roadblock that often plagues teams trying to perform at higher levels.

Maximized Efficiency

We no longer live in a world where the amount of time spent working is an indication of the amount of output that person can produce. This used to be the case 50 years ago. If you were working in a shoe factory, there was no doubt that you would be able to make more shoes working eight hours than you would working five hours. But that is not the case today where a person's output it determined by the efficiency of their work ethic and not the amount of time they spend working.

In 2023 I invested some of my time trying to develop content that we could use as marketing materials. The vision statement for my company was to be the leading authority in business building. I was going to have to create as much content as possible to make this a reality. Here was the problem…. I am not a workaholic and I like to be able to spend time with my family. To me a perfect day is riding my Lamborghini to the park with my wife and kids, walking the dog, having some refreshing drinks, eating pizza on a five-mile walk, enjoying a King of Pops popsicle and coming home just before the sunsets so I can watch it from my porch. None of that involves working or the "grind". So, I was going to have to figure out another way to get this content done without interrupting my time with my family.

A friend of mine had previously mentioned to me that he had a routine of writing 1,000 words per day. I started doing that early in the morning. On some days I would get into flow state, and I could write 3,000 words. On other days it would be a grueling task to get me to 300. But I disciplined myself to do it every day for about 30 minutes to an hour. In a matter of about three year's time period I ended up writing almost 800,000 which I have turned into 14 books. All while not sacrificing anything that I wanted to do with my personal life. I simply became more efficient. With technology the upper limits of your ability to become efficient are not even known but I bet it is ten times more efficient than you are today.

High-performing teams don't waste time or energy. They get in and get out and get the job done before moving on to their next task. You might not need your crew to be the Seal Team Six of businesses, but you also don't want The Three Stooges. For most of us, excellence lies somewhere along that spectrum. In fact, excellence is simply being really good at something for an extended period of time. If you are good at making tacos and you do it for an extended period of time, someone will one day say, "These tacos are excellent."

Communication among team members is key to the efficiency of the team as a whole. If your team communicates not only internally but externally, with other teams, workflows will operate more efficiently with proper communication.

Another way to maximize efficiency in your teams is to be constantly improving the process.

Sir Dave Brailsford

Under the leadership of Sir Dave Brailsford, British Cycling adopted a philosophy known as "marginal gains." The idea was to make tiny improvements in every aspect of cycling, from equipment design to nutrition to training methods, with the belief that these incremental improvements would add up to significant gains overall.

Brailsford and his team implemented rigorous scientific methods to analyze every aspect of the sport, looking for areas where they could gain an edge. This included the design of ergonomic handlebars, optimizing bike fit for each individual rider, and even making sure that they had the best sleep possible.

They developed a culture of excellence through this process. They hired top coaches and staff and worked on instilling a mindset of relentless determination.

The results were unprecedented. The British began to dominate cycling. In the Olympics the British cycling team went on winning multiple gold medals and breaking numerous world records.

All of this brought about by the marginal gains approach.

Cross-Functionality

Cross-functionality refers to one team's ability to work with other teams. This is an especially important cornerstone of high-demand, deadline-oriented work. Consider two separate teams: your paralegal and associate attorney teams. The paralegals must operate in one sphere while the attorneys operate in another. Even though these two separate teams act independently, they must work together to complete the work product. The more seamlessly your team's function across boundaries, the higher the performance will be.

This cross functionality can be found in almost any industry. It is very rare to find a business that does not require cross functional collaboration. Grouping the teams together to create the greatest efficiency is a necessary component to establishing an efficient operation and provide a space for high performing teams to succeed.

Measured Success

The final cornerstone of high-performance teams is found not in their success but in the measure of that success. Many teams perform well, but the highest-performing teams keep outperforming themselves. They thrive on competition. Overcoming challenges are part of their mindset. They may fear but fear does not control them. They shift, pivot, and adapt in one smooth motion, working as one to get the job done. Like the image of a duck floating smoothly on top of a pond, high-performing teams don't always reveal the furious paddling going on under the still waters. You only know the team is performing because the numbers get better and better.

What does it mean to be high performing?

High performing teams want goals and want to be recognized for achieving them. They thrive on excellence and nothing but creating the best outcome is acceptable to them. Every single aspect of their work is dedicated to creating outcomes that beat the previous outcomes.

On this note, remember that measuring the success and failures of your teams is your responsibility. Understand the starting numbers and ending numbers, so you have a way to evaluate your team's performance.

Chapter Takeaway

Ultimately, high performance is a means to an end. Through maximizing efficiency and cross-functionality, you can achieve quantifiable success. If you want a high-performance team, there must be a clear objectively with a quantifiable metric that the members of the team can judge their success. Vague objectives or vague metrics will only lead to an inefficient production and low performance. The more you challenge your team the more likely that you will find the high performers and eliminate the low performers. High performers thrive on the challenges and low performers hide and complain about them.

Chapter 4
Understanding Team Types

"The way a team plays as a whole determines its success. You may have the greatest bunch of individual stars in the world, but if they don't play together, the club won't be worth a dime."

– Babe Ruth

When Apple was getting ready to develop, produce and distribute the iPhone, they did not just use one team to do it all. They had a research and development team, engineering team, software and development team, marketing and sales team, supply chain and manufacturing team, customer service and support team, cross functional collaboration team, and the ongoing innovation and iteration team.

Every team served a different function. Every team was made up of different skill sets. Every team had likely a different unique culture. But together they formed one giant team fully dedicated to the same objective- the release of the iPhone.

Part of your job in building successful teams is understanding what kind of team goes where. Different team structures may work better in different scenarios within the office or even within certain types of offices. Some team types are simply better at performing specific kinds of jobs. One of your tasks in running your own business is learning where to put what kinds of teams. When you accomplish this, you'll be operating at a higher level, and you'll be building high-performing teams along the way.

It is a huge mistake thinking that you can have one team set up for everyone in your business. I see this all the time with business owners who want every department to be run the same. Unfortunately, because the work and skill sets are different, the personality makeups of those department employees will require a different team set up. It's easy to see this by just visualizing the sales team and comparing them to the IT team. If you treated those two teams the same and tried to organize them the same, it is very likely one of the teams would experience high turnover, low production and low engagement.

> *It is a huge mistake thinking that you can have one team set up for everyone in your business.*

Below, I'll discuss some of the most common team types found in businesses or other professional services.

Common Team Type No. 1: Operational Teams

Operational teams help your business operate. These teams oversee office organization and data management systems. They may also coordinate scheduling and travel plans, or any matter pertinent to the daily happenings of your business. When your operations team operates on a high level, you'll see cost savings and experience fewer headaches. Operational teams help create efficiencies in the organization by making sure all aspects of the operations are streamlined and running without friction.

Individuals on operations teams need to be detail-oriented and ready to follow instructions. They should also be great task managers with excellent organization and communication skills. Following a project plan should come as second nature and they should be great at follow through.

Some examples of some common types of business operations teams include:

Supply Chain Management Team: Responsible for managing the flow of goods and services, from sourcing raw materials to delivering finished products to customers.

Logistics Team: Focuses on coordinating the transportation, warehousing, and distribution of goods to ensure timely delivery and cost efficiency.

Production Team: Oversees the manufacturing process, ensuring that products are produced efficiently, meeting quality standards, and optimizing resource utilization.

Quality Assurance (QA) Team: Ensures that products or services meet the specified quality standards through testing, inspection, and implementation of quality control measures.

Customer Service Team: Provides assistance and support to customers before, during, and after the purchase of a product or service, handling inquiries, resolving issues, and ensuring customer satisfaction.

Sales Operations Team: Supports the sales department by managing sales processes, analyzing data, implementing sales strategies, and providing sales support.

Finance and Accounting Team: Manages financial transactions, budgeting, financial reporting, and analysis to support decision-making and ensure financial health and compliance.

Human Resources (HR) Team: Responsible for recruiting, training, managing, and supporting employees, as well as handling HR-related processes such as payroll, benefits administration, and employee relations.

IT Operations Team: Maintains and manages the organization's IT infrastructure, ensuring the availability, reliability, and security of systems and networks.

Business Development Team: Focuses on identifying growth opportunities, forging partnerships, and expanding the organization's market presence through strategic initiatives.

Good business operations teams are essential for the smooth functioning and success of an organization. As you can see from the list above these teams are all different, made up of people with different personalities and educational requirements and serve very distinct purposes within your organization. Here are four key aspects of what good business operations teams do:

1. **Efficiency Optimization**: They constantly seek ways to streamline processes, reduce waste, and improve efficiency across all operational areas of the business. This might involve implementing lean practices, automation, or redesigning workflows.
2. **Resource Management**: They effectively manage resources such as human capital, finances, materials, and equipment to ensure optimal utilization and cost-effectiveness.

3. **Risk Management**: They identify potential risks to the business's operations and develop strategies to mitigate them. This includes anticipating supply chain disruptions, regulatory changes, or other factors that could impact the business.
4. **Continuous Improvement**: They foster a culture of continuous improvement by encouraging feedback, implementing performance metrics, and regularly reviewing processes to identify areas for enhancement.

Common Team Type No. 2: Virtual Teams

There are two types of virtual teams: 1. International virtual assistants and 2. Teams that are U.S. based but work remotely. There are pros and cons of each. Although there are arguments to be made on both sides regarding the pros and cons of virtual teams and the productivity of virtual teams, there is no doubt that the option of a virtual workforce is changing the way people do business.

International virtual teams is changing the landscape of business. Recently I worked with a business that had 80% of their workforce in Colombia. This wasn't a huge conglomerate business with unlimited disposable income. This was a small business that now, through technology, has access to a worldwide workforce.

Virtual teams are increasingly becoming a part of many business environments. Virtual assistant companies seem to be popping up everywhere especially handling all of the back-end work that does not require a front facing environment. For years this sort of help was only available to big companies that could afford to place teams in centers around the world. The world, however, is getting smaller and as more and more people embrace the world workforce, virtual teams are completely changing the landscape of the business world especially in the realm of professional services. Virtual teams aren't great for tasks that need to be handled in-house, so before creating one, figure out what projects you have that lend themselves to a remote setting. One of the major benefits of hiring international virtual assistants is that you can still be incredibly competitive with compensation without breaking the bank. For most countries, paying $10-15 per hour may be 2X the living wage in their country giving US based companies a truly competitive edge.

U.S. based Remote workers often value flexibility in their schedules, so make sure you're clear with your remote teams on your expectations for their schedules. This is especially pertinent if individuals live in different time zones. While the success of remote teams depends in large part on your communication with them, they must also be communicative with you. One of the single most important qualities a remote team is the ability to communicate digitally and be available during work hours.

Common Team Type No. 3: Project-Based Teams

Project-based teams come together to work on special projects, whether client-facing or back-of-house. The nature of the project will determine which employees you choose for the team. While each project and each team is likely to be different from the last, there are ways to build the best high-performance project-based teams possible.

The type of members you choose is important in these scenarios because of the team's parameters. Consider that these teams often last only for the short term; ideally, the people on these teams would be accustomed to hopping from special project to special project. The best project-based team members may be flexible, adaptable, communicative, and ready to jump in and get going.

Common Team Type No. 4: Leadership Teams

I find leadership teams invaluable in all businesses. Leadership teams are more people-oriented than task-oriented. High-performing leadership teams inspire everyone around them through their integrity, loyalty, and commitment. Without a solid leadership team it will be incredibly difficult to grow your organization.

In building your leadership teams, you'll want to pick the individuals who either have proven leadership skills or who are eager to acquire them. Implementing an entire leadership program into your practice may prove an excellent way of simultaneously honing these skills and boosting team performance at every level.

Chapter Takeaway

Your teams need to be filled with the right people performing the right types of tasks. Not all teams are the same or for the same purpose. Identifying how to group team members so that they form the most cohesive team for a project is an invaluable skill set for your organization. Regardless of the differences in your teams, they must be aligned on the same objective to effectively win. Without teams your company is missing a secret ingredient to growth.

Chapter 5
Team Member Values

"Nothing can stop the man with the right mental attitude from achieving his goal; nothing on earth can help the man with the wrong mental attitude."

–Thomas Jefferson

One of my favorite movies ever to watch was "Lone Survivor". This is a true story of survival, resilience, and brotherhood in the face of overwhelming odds. The account is based on the experiences of Marcus Luttrell, a former United States Navy SEAL, during Operation Red Wings in Afghanistan in 2005.

Marcus Luttrell, along with three fellow SEAL team members - Michael Murphy, Danny Dietz, and Matthew Axelson - were deployed on a mission to capture/kill a high-ranking Taliban leader. The operation was compromised when they encountered a group of Afghan goat herders. At first, they did not want to let the goat herders go because they believed if they did, their location would be disclosed. However, one of the herders was a young boy and they ultimately decided to let the boy go.

Shortly after releasing the goat herders, the herders alerted the Taliban to their location and they found themselves surrounded. A firefight ensued, and Dietz, Murphy, and Axelson all died in the gun battle. Luttrell, the lone survivor, suffered severe injuries but managed to evade capture and was ultimately helped by Afghan villagers who risked their lives to protect him from the Taliban.

The movie highlights the bravery, sacrifice, and camaraderie of the SEAL team members, who remained steadfast in their commitment to each other and their mission until the very end. The movie is all about the shared values that exist in the military and specifically the within the Navy SEALS.

So far, we've been thinking about the team as a whole. At this point, you should have a solid understanding of what to look for when evaluating the performance of your teams. Now I want to shift gears and talk about individual personalities on your teams. There is more to building high-performing teams than (1) knowing what you want your team to accomplish and (2) knowing what kind of teams need to be placed where. You also want to make sure the values of your team members align.

The values of the team will help drive the team to success when there are disagreements about how to achieve an objective. When teams do not share the same values for work ethic, ambition, excellence, etc. you may find members of the team frustrated at others for not pulling their weight.

There are a couple of questions you should be asking when you build out your teams. Are the values of individual team members compatible with those of the other members? Are they consistent with your company culture? While diverse points of view can make teams stronger and more effective, disagreement on fundamentals can create conflict and even gridlock. The key is to know your people, communicate with them openly and often, and keep the team's objectives clear.

When teams do not share the same values for work ethic, ambition, excellence, etc. you may find members of the team frustrated at others for not pulling their weight.

Core Values

Members of high-performing teams often share similar backgrounds and worldviews. Members of other high-performing teams come together from more diverse backgrounds and experiences, and see the world in vastly different terms. Both of these scenarios have been part of my professional career, and both are backed by academic studies.

Diverse personal and professional histories and cultures can combine to produce ingenuity and creative problem-solving. But if team members don't share similar values, diversity can also create conflict. Values sharing is the critical component that drives diverse teams through to success.

I have been blessed over the years to have a great team that loves working together. No matter where I have led, it seems like the people that worked closest to me have always gelled together really well. Recently I was at a team meeting with my leadership team and a topic was brought up that many times is deemed to be controversial in most work environments. To my surprise all 6 people in attendance were all on the same page. I was stunned. The 6 people were white and latino, men and women, older and younger and YET they all seemed to agree on an issue. When I began to analyze why, I realized it was because of the shared values we had about life. The key to building a high performance team is a tremendous amount of alignment in the values of the organization regardless of the demographic diversity that might exist.

The core values that matter for your teams might include a sense of fairness and honesty, a strong work ethic, and the importance of listening. Personal priorities such as the importance of travel, family, or environmental stewardship might play a role here, too. Employees don't have to be from the same walk of life to share values. I have seen this play out time and time again.

The SEALS have core values summarized by an acronym TRIDENT—Teamwork, Resilience, Integrity, Devotion to Duty, Excellence, Non-quitting spirit and trust. Everyone that is a member of the SEALS, regardless of their background and what they look like, race, race color or gender, all must share these values to ensure the team is high performing. All of these values were exhibited by Luttrell as an individual for the benefit of his team.

How Values Drive Performance

Values often drive performance. If your teams share core values that prioritize deadlines over the quality of the work, you might get your projects done on time, but not at the level you expect from your firm. If the values are reversed, you could end up with an excellent work product that's always a week late. This, too, is problematic. The point is, when it comes to workplace values, the values of individual team members should complement those of the others, and bring out everyone's best.

In building high-performance teams, try to put individuals together whose values create synergy. You could pair deadline-oriented people with work-quality-oriented people, for instance—but be careful not to position two polar opposites against one another, as that's a recipe for conflict.

Consider asking team members to take an Enneagram test, so you can learn how to best partner them up for values-based compatibility. If you choose to do this, make sure you educate yourself on the Enneagram and understand how best to use the results of the assessments.

Communicating Your Company Values

It's important for your team members to share the same or complementary values to avoid conflict, but it's also just as important that they share these qualities with your company. Different companies have different cultures. Some big businesses like to promote a brand of aggressive advocacy, while others would rather cater to the free-spirited entrepreneur. Your brand is up to you, but you must ensure that the values you prioritize effectively convey your company culture.

If you fail to communicate your company values, your teams will suffer. They won't suffer because they are bad teams; they'll suffer because they aren't performing in a way that aligns with your ultimate vision and goals.

Chapter Takeaway

High-performance teams share values with the company and among their teammates. Values cross diversity lines, and ideal teammates share values that complement each other without causing conflict.

Chapter 6
Earning Trust

"Trust is not something you build. It's something you earn. You can choose to act trustworthy by demonstrating your integrity, benevolence, and reliability. But it's up to others to grant you trust—and it's up to you to keep earning it."

– Adam Grant

The Battle of Trenton 1776.

I absolutely love the period of the American Revolution. After watching the Broadway Play Hamilton I was hooked on the stories of the early Americans who created this amazing country.

One particular story that I loved of that time period, was the Battle of Trenton. George Washington was a couple of battles away from being just another general that died in battle. But everything changed in the Battle of Trenton. After suffering a series of defeats,

General Washington and his Continental Army found themselves in dire straits. Washington's army was outnumbered and outmanned, ill-equipped to face the British forces.

Facing the prospect of defeat, Washington devised a plan to launch a surprise attack on the forces stationed in Trenton, New Jersey, on the morning of December 26, 1776. Despite the harsh winter conditions and the risks involved, Washington placed his trust in his troops and their ability to execute the plan.

During the daring crossing of the ice-clogged Delaware River on Christmas night, Washington's trust in his troops was put to the test. It was such a dangerous crossing that two detachments were unable to cross the river, leaving Washington with only 2,400 men under his command in the assault, 3,000 fewer than planned. Despite the logistical challenges, the Continental Army successfully navigated the river and launched a surprise attack on the unsuspecting Hessian mercenaries, who were caught off guard and quickly overwhelmed.

The victory at the Battle of Trenton was a pivotal turning point in the Revolutionary War, boosting morale among American forces and demonstrating to both the Continental Army and the public that victory against the British was possible. Washington's decision to trust his troops and their ability to execute a daring plan under difficult circumstances played a crucial role in the success of the operation.

The Battle of Trenton bolstered the confidence of the Continental Army but also solidified Washington's reputation as a decisive and effective military leader. His willingness to place his trust in his troops and lead by example inspired loyalty and devotion among his soldiers, laying the foundation for future victories in the fight for American independence.

A very special glue often bonds high-performing teams. That glue is trust. And trust is an extremely powerful glue. It can help overcome almost all problems in a team. With trust men and women are willing to die for each other.

However, a team without trust cannot perform at a high level, if at all. When teammates don't trust one another, individuals become alienated and may even fear the others are out to harm them. Instead of performing work that impacts the overall goal, they are more interested in self-preservation. Trust is a critical foundation for high-performing teams.

You must prioritize and foster trust at every stage of team operations. You must recognize that trust can be fragile. It is easy to break and takes a long time to develop or mend. In this chapter, I'll discuss some of the best methods for fostering trust while building high-performing teams.

Trust Tip #1: Avoid the Blame Game

Here is the bottom line: something is going to go wrong. In fact, something always goes wrong. There is no way to avoid making mistakes in this game of business. The absolute worst possible thing you can do is start the blame game. I used to work with a colleague that nothing was ever his fault. He blamed other employees, leaders and vendors. He was not responsible for anything even when he was completely responsible for the decision being made.

Trust is an extremely powerful glue. It can help overcome almost all problems in a team. With trust men and women are willing to die for each other.

The best-performing teams avoid blaming each other when things go wrong. Blaming others is an easy habit to fall into and, honestly, people do sometimes drop the ball. If a project misses a deadline because a teammate failed to do their part, it seems only fair that the other team members would and should point the finger, right? Wrong.

First, upper management wants results, not the blame game. More importantly, however, blaming others doesn't foster trust among the team. In fact, it erodes it. When someone drops the ball, teammates should have an open and honest discussion with that person. If the problem persists, the team members should have a clear roadmap of procedures that helps everyone feel safe.

The colleague I mentioned above was trusted by no one. Everyone always thought he was out to get them. This environment does not create a trusting organization.

Trust Tip #2: Encourage Honesty

Several years ago I was working with a client that had a trusted employee overseeing the building project in the business. This employee worked for the organization for almost 5 years. In that time period, they had become a trusted employee even coming over for dinners and enjoying time with the family.

In the building project capacity, this employee was able to write checks to vendors. Due to a lack of integrity, the employee was able to write checks to themselves to the tune of over $100,000. The business owner was devasted. Immediately she wanted to retake control of finances and not let anyone touch it. She started questioning everything in the business. It greatly eroded her trust in not only the employee but people in general.

You must encourage honesty amongst the team if you want to create a high trust organization. This sounds like almost common sense but it's not. You have to tell adults to be honest. Believe it or not, it is part of the human condition to lie. Honesty, however, is mandatory in trust building, full stop. Without honesty, everyone on the team is apt to fall into old habits of self-preservation. Honesty in teamwork looks like this:

- Owning mistakes
- Owning a lack of knowledge
- Owning a bad attitude
- Owning areas that need improvement

Honesty is about being forthcoming and placing the highest importance on the team's health. It's much more important than individual egos. Honesty begets honesty.

Trust Tip #3: Promote Bonding Opportunities

All too often you hear about companies that pride themselves at keeping work at work and private life private. Unfortunately, it's harder to build trust in that environment.

I have a distinct disadvantage in building my business because we host conferences 4 times per year and every employee is required to attend. The conferences are always in different places and the team has to travel to get there. These experiences always create an incredible bonding experience for the team and fosters a tremendous amount of trust for one another.

Trust often relies on shared experiences. Sometimes these shared experiences come from being raised with similar backgrounds or going through a similar educational process. Other times, these shared experiences develop in the workplace. If you're in charge of developing high-performance teams, you should make sure you're giving the team members ample time to bond through shared experiences.

Team building events can be big, highly planned experiences or small ice-breaker-type moments peppered in throughout the week. Bonding and shared experiences help teammates acknowledge one another's individuality and humanity. Try a group lunch, dinner or happy hour. Get the extended family involved. It is more likely that we will trust someone that we know and like.

Trust Tip #4: Stop Moving the Goal Posts

I remember working with a leader once that was constantly moving the goal post. No matter what target you hit, it was never enough. The constant negativity began to wear on me to the point that I began to not trust that this person had my best interest in mind. Even though I was a high producer, my performance started to taper off when I realized nothing was ever going to satisfy this leader.

If you're in charge of building high-performance teams at your firm, there are steps you can take to reinforce trust. As I said, trust begets trust, and if it doesn't start at the top, you're doomed. Your teams must trust you. There are several ways a manager or firm owner can jeopardize trust. One common and seemingly innocent way is indecision. Indecision will manifest as a constant moving of the goalposts.

Your teams need to know what they're working toward if you want them to perform at high levels. You can't give them one objective on day one and change it on day ten. If you do, they'll constantly second-guess you and distrust your directions.

Chapter Takeaway

Building trust requires humility and honesty. Trust begets trust, and the more you give, often the more you'll get. Without trust you can't build a high-performance team. With trust, your team becomes unstoppable and can overcome all the odds it may face.

Chapter 7
Clarity and Communication

"Nothing in life is more important than the ability to communicate effectively."

– Gerald R. Ford

In 1982, the NY Giants were in their 58th season of football. The head coach was Ray Perkins and he was in his fourth season. That year the season was shortened due to a player strike and finished with a 4-5 record. In four years, he had a record of 23 wins and 34 losses. At the end of the season, he left for the University of Alabama and was replaced with what would become one of the most legendary coaches of all time, Bill Parcells.

In his book, "Finding a way to Win" Parcells wrote, "Explain what you're trying to accomplish...when people understand the point of the risk, they're more likely to give their all, in the effort, and less likely to second-guess afterward... Establish clear expectations – people can't become accountable unless they understand exactly what you want."

In 1983, the young Parcells led the New York Giants through an abysmal season—winning only three games. In the next six seasons however, his NY giants climbed to the top of the league, winning three division titles and two Super Bowls. He then became coach of the New England Patriots in 1993. They were coming off two years in which they had won a combined total of three games. Yet in 1996, they were in the Super Bowl.

> *Ambiguity and indecision are the enemies of productivity, and these bad habits abound in the workplace.*

Then in 1997, when he arrived to the New York Jets. The team had just suffered through a 1–15 season. Two years later, he made it to the conference championship.

Overall he had 172-130 record and is the only coach in NFL history to take four teams to the playoffs and three to the conference championship game. All because he was clear about what he expected from his players, his coaches, and the organization.

Good teams will operate under almost any directive, but high-performing teams operate best under *clear* directives and *clear* communication. Ambiguity and indecision are the enemies of productivity, and these bad habits abound in the workplace. You can improve clarity and communication at your firm by ensuring you have great communicators in charge of your teams. Putting the right people in charge isn't always intuitive, and many managers make the mistake of putting their most innovative thinkers at the helm.

While no one can fault you for wanting to put a great mind in charge of your teams, you need to ask whether that great mind is the right kind. Big-picture thinkers often fail as leaders because they don't communicate clearly. High-performing teams and their leaders exhibit a triad of strengths: defined responsibilities, communication, and feedback.

1. Defined Responsibilities

Your teams need to have defined responsibilities to function at the highest levels. This can be more difficult to achieve than you might imagine. Poorly defined duties can mean team members find ways to shirk their duties, or it can mean they end up taking on more than their share of the workload. Either way, there's a loss of efficiency, as two people perform the same task twice or a task is neglected entirely. These oversights and redundancies don't occur when roles are clearly established and defined.

As you build your high-performance teams, ensure you've written out the scope of every participant's role. Including visual aids, like Venn diagrams, can be helpful in weeding out overlap. Make sure you revisit these roles at least every few months.

2. Open Communication

Even the most transparent of managers can see communication breakdowns at their firm. This is because they don't account for the flow of communication that needs to come back to them. Too often, communication only flows from the top down. High-performing teams communicate in all directions. The best organizations will communicate direction down to their teams and will solicit feedback up so that there is continuous loop of communication at all times.

You can define the roles on your teams all day long, but if there isn't clear communication flowing in all directions, your teams will falter. There are many ways you can foster healthy communication between team members and leadership. Teams and their leaders, at every level, should practice and promote effective:

- Verbal communication, such as tone of voice, meeting etiquette, phone calls, and remote conferencing.
- Physical communication, such as eye contact, body language, gestures, and expressions.

- Written communication, such as emails, intra-office chat, and intraoffice paperwork or reports.

Listening is a critically important component of effective communication. Great listeners will practice repeating what's been said to them to ensure they understand the directive.

3. Unambiguous Feedback

Feedback is often too overlooked in the workplace. It may be that your office practices giving feedback only when things go wrong, but you should consider using feedback as a more versatile tool. Let your teams know when they've done a good job, and let them know when they've done an okay job. High-performing teams crave feedback, and they deserve to know when there's room for improvement or when they've hit the project out of the ballpark. Likewise, leaders should ask for feedback from their teams. Feedback that flows both ways allows everyone the opportunity to improve when necessary.

Chapter Takeaway

Clarity is about making sure everyone knows what, how, and why. What is their job? How should they perform the duties of their job? Why is their role scoped the way it is? Ultimately, the big picture and the smaller picture of a person's role within a team should align without confusion. Communication is a two-way street. Remember you need to do more than give feedback when something goes wrong; you need to provide a channel where communication can flow both ways.

Chapter 8
Developing Leadership

"Leadership is about making others better as a result of your presence and making sure that impact lasts in your absence."

— Sheryl Sandberg

Founded by Yvon Chouinard in 1973, Patagonia started as a small climbing equipment company in California. It has evolved into a globally recognized outdoor apparel and gear brand known for its commitment to environmental sustainability and social responsibility.

Yvon Chouinard's leadership style, characterized by a strong focus on environmental ethics and employee empowerment, has been instrumental in shaping Patagonia's success. Under his guidance, Patagonia has implemented groundbreaking initiatives such as using recycled materials in its products, supporting environmental activism, and donating a portion of its profits to grassroots environmental organizations.

Chouinard's emphasis on creating a company culture has not only attracted top talent but also fostered a sense of purpose and commitment among employees. Patagonia has been consistently recognized as one of the best places to work. The company's dedication to its core values, coupled with Chouinard's visionary leadership, has enabled Patagonia to thrive as a small company while making a significant impact on environmental conservation and social justice issues globally.

Leadership is paramount in building high-performance teams. If the collective body of team members is the boat, then the leader is the captain. The leader of your teams is responsible for steering the ship and ensuring everyone arrives where they're supposed to on time. When you begin building your teams, you may not have a candidate that stands out to you as a great leader. The good news is that you can help develop leadership qualities in your employees at every level.

> *If the collective body of team members is the boat, then the leader is the captain.*

There's tremendous value in cultivating leaders within your workforce. Not only does the interest you take in helping employees develop this skill promote loyalty, it also provides you with an abundance of talent to choose from in building your teams.

Leadership Hierarchies

Effective leadership accomplishes more than you might initially guess. Great leaders help steer your teams and instill loyalty among team members. Leaders are the reflection of the ownership and they should pass down the work ethic and values expected from the organization. Teams perform at high levels when they feel they're part of a bigger picture and shared cause. This kind of cohesion builds a drive within each person that compels them to do their best work. They aren't just performing for their own benefit; they're performing for the benefit of their teammates and the company.

> *Leaders are the reflection of the ownership and they should pass down the work ethic and values expected from the organization.*

To implement effective leadership at every level of your business, create hierarchies. Consider this: you're the leader of everyone at your business, but that doesn't mean you can build the type of personal relationships that foster loyalty with every single person. Realistically, you can build that bond with only a handful of individuals. My experience is that you can only build this effectively with about 7-10 people. If you're planning on expansive growth, you simply won't have the capacity or hours in the day to be everyone's direct leader.

Instead, you'll be the direct leader of your top managers, and each of those managers will be the leader of a group further down the employment chain. These leadership hierarchies will help you develop loyalty in your teams at every level, from the data entry clerk to the senior associate. Whatever you do and teach is what your leaders will emulate.

Internal Leadership Programs

Although you want your teams to focus on their work-related tasks, you can also cultivate high-performance teams through leadership programs that don't relate to their current jobs. I have implemented an internal leadership program at my business in the past that required all leaders to attend 4-6 hours per year for all employees. As part of my consulting group, I have created a 36 week leadership academy. I appreciate being able to help those who show initiative and want to grow their skillset. At the same time, I'm developing leaders in-house, and when the time comes for them to step into bigger roles with more responsibility, I can hire internally to build my teams.

Utilize Outside Leadership Experts

In addition to your internal leadership programs, you should also integrate outside leadership experts into your curriculum. I like to host monthly leadership meetings, and I'll often bring in a guest speaker to motivate the crew with insightful lessons. I'll make this monthly opportunity available to anyone who wants to participate in my leadership programs.

Those who've advanced in my leadership training opportunities get to go a step further. Each year, when employees achieve the necessary benchmarks in my program, they get to attend a firm-sponsored leadership conference. This is a valuable and fun experience for these employees, but it's also more than that. I see a significant return on investment because these leaders bring back new skills that contribute to the teams' high performance.

Chapter Takeaway

Leadership skills are crucial in empowering teams to operate at their highest levels. Empowered teams operate at peak performance because they function, in large part, on loyalty to one another and the company. Their successes are everyone's successes. Focus on developing your leadership to experience fast and sustained growth.

Chapter 9
Team Building

"If you can laugh together, you can work together."

— Robert Orben

I've saved the "Team Building" chapter of this book for last because there's so much to it. Team building is crucial because it fosters congeniality, goodwill, patience, and friendship. Fun team-building experiences break the ice between new and old members, and deepen the bonds of existing teams.

Bottom-line focused firm managers are sometimes reluctant to allocate time and budgets for what seems to them like a frivolous waste of resources. They mistakenly think high performance is all work and no play—and that play has no deeper meaning. These assumptions are incorrect; the bonds among members of high-performing teams are the foundation of every other principle in this book. Loyalty and friendship foster trust and communication, leading to excellent performance.

How Much to Budget for Team Building

That said, spending on team-building activities can easily spiral out of control, so it's always best to plan for these events with an allocated budget. In addition to the per-person cost of the activities, you need to consider the opportunity costs of taking your team off-task for a long lunch or an entire workday. There is no shortage of team-building activities if you do some research, ranging from lavish companywide retreats to icebreakers you can do before your weekly meetings.

Ultimately, a good rule of thumb is that you can expect to spend about $50-$100 per person for most team-building activities. Some other metrics could be a percentage of revenue. In some industries spending 2% of revenue on employee engagement is another way of measuring the spend.

How Often Do You Team Build?

How often you do team-building activities is ultimately up to you and your budget. For bigger events, like retreats or another activity you'd close the office down for, you'll probably want to limit those experiences to annual events. You can pepper in smaller occasions between big team-building events as needed. Remember that team building doesn't just allow your teams the opportunity to bond and develop friendships; it's also just a fun thing to look forward to. Little breaks can go a long way in boosting morale, which further drives teams to perform at the highest levels possible.

Research has shown that you should strive for no less than one activity every 90 days. Most people lose their energy every quarter and this will help you keep the spirit alive and everyone excited about the future of the company.

Team Building for Virtual Employees

Last but not least, we need to talk about those employees who might need team building the most but are the hardest to bring together—the virtual teams. These days, virtual teams can be a significant asset to your workforce, but, like all teams, they need to develop a sense of loyalty and community if they're going to perform at the highest levels possible.

Several years ago, you'd have had a hard time finding ways to boost remote worker engagement, but in a post-pandemic world, most companies have had to come up with creative team-building experiences online. These can include funny home tours or virtual scavenger hunts. If your remote teams don't often meet through video conferencing, you can host a virtual happy hour. Some remote workers may live in the same city—if that's the case, you could sponsor an in-person activity. With a little creativity and a quick google search, you'll easily find team-building activities for virtual employees. Virtual teams benefit just as much from fun, bonding experiences as in-person teams do.

Chapter Takeaway

Prioritize team building in person and for your virtual employees. To successfully implement team-building activities, build a budget and a consistent schedule to give teams something to look forward to. Team building creates strong teams, and strong teams perform better.

Conclusion

"Believe you can and you are halfway there."

– Theodore Roosevelt

There is an art to building high-performance teams. Throughout my years as a managing partner of a couple fast-growing law firms and now as a consultant of a national consulting firm, I know that 8-Figure Firm level growth requires your teams to work like well-oiled machines. This is partly because you need them to handle a growing workload. But it's also because you need them to seamlessly integrate new team members as you add employees. Getting the actual work done is only half of the job. In many respects, the rest of the job is making certain operational functions are firing on all cylinders.

I wrote this book to share with you what I know about building high-performance teams. Through my own experience and mistakes, I've learned what helps and what makes an issue worse. I want to be the voice that helps you make the right decisions and avoid those missteps that can be costly and demoralizing. In doing so, we discussed the following:

- How to recognize underperforming teams before you can start building high-performance teams.
- What high-performance means in terms of ideal teams and firm management.
- Why you need to recognize the various types of teams you can have in your firm and where best to utilize them.
- How team member values affect performance.
- The critical importance of building trust among teammates.
- Why high-performance teams need clarity and communication to reach peak performance.
- How leadership impacts team performance.
- When and how to implement team building activities.

Once you've completed your reading of *Building High-Performance Teams*, you'll be able to put employees together in ways you hadn't considered before. You'll be able to build your best teams possible. In using this book, you can apply lessons from the chapters individually, or you can take a comprehensive approach to implementing all the suggestions.

Conclusion

One of the biggest things I've learned in my career is that often, success is achieved through determination and an unwillingness to stop trying.

If you're on the cusp of really growing your business, you know you need your teams in top working order. Hopefully, you're reading this in preparation for a big growth initiative, but even if you aren't, you can still course correct. One of the biggest things I've learned in my career is that often, success is achieved through determination and an unwillingness to stop trying. It's never too late to pick up this book and begin your journey toward building high-performance teams.

While there's plenty of information out there regarding how to build perfect teams, a lot of it's geared toward business owners who are just starting out or who are managing big corporate teams for giant companies. I wanted to provide a guide that fills the space between those two niches. This guide is for established firms who've had success but are ready to fine-tune their practices in a way that brings huge growth. I'm uniquely qualified to write just this sort of guide because I've lived it!

While growth and building high-performance teams can seem like an insurmountable task, it can be done. I know this because I've done it, and you can too!

Building High Performance Teams

Team Exercise Questions

1. What are the core values and goals of the team, and how effectively have I communicated them to ensure alignment?

2. How well do I know the strengths and weaknesses of each team member, and how am I leveraging their individual skills to maximize overall team performance?

3. Am I fostering an environment of trust and psychological safety where team members feel comfortable sharing ideas and taking risks?

4. How effective is the current communication structure, and are there any barriers that might be hindering open and efficient dialogue?

5. Am I providing the right balance of guidance and autonomy, allowing team members to take ownership while also offering support when needed?

6. How do I handle conflicts or disagreements within the team, and are there strategies in place to resolve issues constructively?

7. What mechanisms are in place to regularly assess and improve team performance, and how actively do I engage in this process?

8. How well am I recognizing and rewarding the contributions and achievements of team members?

9. Am I adaptable and open to feedback from the team, and how do I incorporate their input into team development strategies?

10. What strategies do I have in place for professional development, and how am I supporting team members in their growth and career aspirations?

11. What is missing in my team that may be able to create more alignment amongst the members of the team?

12. If trust is the glue, how do I make my team stickier?

13. Where have I failed in creating clarity, alignment and trust?

14. How can I be more intentional in developing my team and fostering an environment that promotes high performance?

www.ingramcontent.com/pod-product-compliance
Lightning Source LLC
Chambersburg PA
CBHW070347230526
45471CB00006B/2456